# Bloodlines

*The Wesleyan Poetry Program: Volume 77*

# BLOOD-
# LINES

by
Charles Wright

Wesleyan University Press
Middletown, Connecticut

Acknowledgement is gratefully made to the following periodicals, in the pages of which all the poems in this book were first published: *The American Poetry Review (Tattoos)*; *The Barataria Review* ('Easter, 1974'); *Lillabulero* ('Delta Traveller'); *The New Yorker* ('Rural Route'); *The Ohio Review* ('Bays Mountain Covenant', 'Cancer Rising' and 'Virgo Descending'); *The Partisan Review* ('Link Chain'); *Poetry (Skins)*; and *The Southern Poetry Review* ('Hardin County').

**Library of Congress Cataloging in Publication Data**

Wright, Charles, 1935–
  Bloodlines.

  (The Wesleyan poetry program: v. 77)
  I. Title
PS3573.R52B5      811'.5'4      74-23289
ISBN 0-8195-2077-2
ISBN 0-8195-1077-7 pbk.

Manufactured in the United States of America
First edition

*For Winter Wright*

# Contents

1.

## Virgo Descending

Through the viridian (and black of the burnt match),
Through ox-blood and ochre, the ham-colored clay,
Through plate after plate, down
Where the worm and the mole will not go,
Through ore-seam and fire-seam,
My grandmother, senile and 89, crimpbacked, stands
Like a door ajar on her soft bed,
The open beams and bare studs of the hall
Pink as an infant's skin in the floating dark;
Shavings and curls swing down like snowflakes across her face.

My aunt and I walk past. As always, my father
Is planning rooms, dragging his lame leg,
Stroke-straightened and foreign, behind him,
An aberrant 2-by-4 he can't fit snug.
I lay my head on my aunt's shoulder, feeling
At home, and walk on.
Through arches and door jambs, the spidery wires
And coiled cables, the blueprint takes shape:
My mother's room to the left, the door closed;
My father's room to the left, the door closed—

Ahead, my brother's room, unfinished;
Behind, my sister's room, also unfinished.
Buttresses, winches, block-and-tackle: the scale of everything
Is enormous. We keep on walking. And pass
My aunt's room, almost complete, the curtains up,
The lamp and the medicine arranged
In their proper places, in arm's reach of where the bed will go . . .

The next one is mine, now more than half done,
Cloyed by the scent of jasmine,
White-gummed and anxious, their mouths sucking the air dry.

Home is what you lie in, or hang above, the house
Your father made, or keeps on making,
The dirt you moisten, the sap you push up and nourish . . .
I enter the living room, it, too, unfinished, its far wall
Not there, opening on to a radiance
I can't begin to imagine, a light
My father walks from, approaching me,
Dragging his right leg, rolling his plans into a perfect curl.
That light, he mutters, that damned light.
We can't keep it out. It keeps on filling your room.

## Easter, 1974

Against the tin roof of the back porch, the twilight
Backdrops the climbing rose, three
Blood stars, redemptive past pain.

Trust in the fingernail, the eyelash,
The bark that channels the bone.
What opens will close, what hungers is what goes half-full.

## Cancer Rising

It starts with a bump, a tiny bump, deep in the throat.
The mockingbird knows: she spreads it around
Like music, like something she's heard, a gossip to be
Repeated, but not believed.
And the bump grows, and the song grows, the song
Ascendant and self-reflective, its notes
Obscuring the quarter-tone, the slick flesh and the burning.
And the bump drops off and disappears, but
Its roots do not disappear — they dig on through the moist meat.

The roots are worms, worms in a cheese.
And what they leave, in their blind passage,
Filtered, reorganized, is a new cheese, a cheese
For one palate and one tongue.
But this takes time, and comes later,
The small mounds, heaps of a requisite sorrow,
Choked and grown in the beds,
The channels no longer channels, but flesh of a kind
Themselves, the same flesh and the song . . .

Midnight again, the mockingbird, high
In the liquidambar, runs through her scales. What burdens
Down-shift and fall, their weights sprung:
The start, the rise, the notes
Oil for the ear of death, oil for the wind, the corpse
Sailing into the universe, the geranium . . .
The music, like high water, rises inexorably . . .
Toward heaven, that intergalactic queasiness
Where all fall to the same riff.

Tallow, tallow and ash. The fire winds
Like a breath through the bone, a common tune,
Hummable, hard to extrapolate:
That song again, the song of burnt notes.
The blue it rises into, the cobalt,
Proves an enduring flame: Persian death bowl,
The bead, crystal
And drowned delta, Ephesian reed.
Blue of the twice-bitten rose, blue of the dove . . .

## Tattoos

                1.

Necklace of flame, little dropped hearts,
Camellias: I crunch you under my foot.
And here comes the wind again, bad breath
Of thirty-odd years, and catching up. Still,
I crunch you under my foot.

Your white stalks sequester me,
Their roots a remembered solitude.
Their mouths of snow keep forming my name.
Programmed incendiaries,
Fused flesh, so light your flowering,

So light the light that fires you
—Petals of horn, scales of blood—,
Where would you have me return?
What songs would I sing,
And the hymns . . . What garden of wax statues . . .

                                        *1973*

2.

The pin oak has found new meat,
The linkworm a bone to pick.
Lolling its head, slicking its blue tongue,
The nightflower blooms on its one stem;
The crabgrass hones down its knives:

Between us again there is nothing. And since
The darkness is only light
That has not yet reached us,
You slip it on like a glove.
*Duck soup*, you say. *This is duck soup.*

And so it is.
            Along the far bank
Of Blood Creek, I watch you turn
In that light, and turn, and turn,
Feeling it change on your changing hands,
Feeling it take. Feeling it.

*1972*

3.

Body fat as my forearm, blunt-arrowed head
And motionless, eyes
Sequin and hammer and nail
In the torchlight, he hangs there,
Color of dead leaves, color of dust,

Dumbbell and hourglass — copperhead.
Color of bread dough, color of pain, the hand
That takes it, that handles it
— The snake now limp as a cat —
Is halfway to heaven, and in time.

Then Yellow Shirt, twitching and dancing,
Gathers it home, handclap and heartstring,
His habit in ecstasy.
Current and godhead, hot coil,
Grains through the hourglass glint and spring.

*1951*

4.

Silt fingers, silt stump and bone.
And twice now, in the drugged sky,
*White moons, black moons.*
And twice now, in the gardens,
The great seed of affection.

Liplap of Zuan's canal, blear
Footfalls of Tintoretto; the rest
Is brilliance: Turner at 3 a. m.; moth lamps
Along the casements. O blue
Feathers, this clear cathedral . . .

And now these stanchions of joy,
Radiant underpinning:
Old scaffolding, old arrangements,
All fall in a rain of light.
I have seen what I have seen.

*1968*

5.

Hungering acolyte, pale body,
The sunlight — through St Paul of the 12 Sorrows —
Falls like Damascus òn me:
I feel the gold hair of Paradise rise through my skin
Needle and thread, needle and thread;

I feel the worm in the rose root.
I hear the river of heaven
Fall from the air. I hear it enter the wafer
And sink me, the whirlpool stars
Spinning me down, and down. O . . .

Now I am something else, smooth,
Unrooted, with no veins and no hair, washed
In the waters of nothingness;
Anticoronal, released . . .
And then I am risen, the cup, new sun, at my lips.

*1946*

6.

Skyhooked above the floor, sucked
And mummied by salt towels, my left arm
Hangs in the darkness, bloodwood, black gauze,
The slow circle of poison
Coming and going through the same hole . . .

Sprinkle of rain through the pine needles,
Shoosh pump shoosh pump of the heart;
Bad blood, bad blood . . .
                        Chalk skin like a light,
Eyes thin dimes, whose face
Comes and goes at the window?

Whose face . . .
            For I would join it,
And climb through the nine-and-a-half footholds of fever
Into the high air,
And shed these clothes and renounce,
Burned over, repurified.

*1941*

7.

This one's not like the other, pale, gingerly—
Like nothing, in fact, to rise, as he does,
In three days, his blood clotted,
His deathsheet a feather across his chest,
His eyes twin lenses, and ready to unroll.

Arm and a leg, nail hole and knucklebone,
He stands up. In his right hand,
The flagstaff of victory;
In his left, the folds of what altered him.
And the hills spell V, and the trees V . . .

Nameless, invisible, what spins out
From this wall comes breath by breath,
And pulls the vine, and the ringing tide,
The scorched syllable from the moon's mouth.
And what pulls them pulls me.

*1963*

8.

A tongue hangs in the dawn wind, a wind
That trails the tongue's voice like a banner, star
And whitewash, the voice
Sailing across the 14 mountains, snap and drift,
To settle, a last sigh, here.

That tongue is his tongue, the voice his voice:
Lifting out of the sea
Where the tongue licks, the voice starts,
Monotonous, out of sync,
*Yarmulke, tfillin, tallis,*

His nude body waist-deep in the waves,
The book a fire in his hands, his movements
Reedflow and counter flow, the chant light
From his lips, the prayer rising to heaven,
And everything brilliance, brilliance, brilliance.

*1959*

9.

In the fixed crosshairs of evening,
In the dust-wallow of certitude,
Where the drop drops and the scalding starts,
Where the train pulls out and the light winks,
The tracks go on, and go on:

The flesh pulls back and snaps,
The fingers are ground and scraped clean,
Reed whistles in a green fire.
The bones blow on, singing their bald song.
It stops. And it starts again.

Theologians, Interpreters:
Song, the tracks, crosshairs, the light;
The drop that is always falling.
Over again I feel the palm print,
The map that will take me there.

*1952*

10.

It starts here, in a chair, sunflowers
Inclined from an iron pot, a soiled dishcloth
Draped on the backrest. A throat with a red choker
Throbs in the mirror. High on the wall,
Flower-like, disembodied,

A wren-colored evil eye stares out
At the white blooms of the oleander, at the white
Gobbets of shadow and shade,
At the white lady and white parasol, at this
Dichogamous landscape, this found chord

(And in the hibiscus and moonflowers,
In the smoke trees and spider ferns,
The unicorn crosses his thin legs,
The leopard sips at her dish of blood,
And the vines strike and the vines recoil).

*1973*

11.

So that was it, the rush and the take-off,
The oily glide of the cells
Bringing it up — ripsurge, refraction,
The inner spin
Trailing into the cracked lights of oblivion . . .

Re-entry is something else, blank, hard:
Black stretcher straps; the peck, peck
And click of a scalpel; glass shards
Eased one by one from the flesh;
Recisions; the long bite of the veins . . .

And what do we do with this,
Rechuted, reworked into our same lives, no one
To answer to, no one to glimpse and sing,
The cracked light flashing our names?
We stand fast, friend, we stand fast.

*1958*

12.

Oval oval oval oval push pull push pull . . .
Words unroll from our fingers.
A splash of leaves through the windowpanes,
A smell of tar from the streets:
Apple, arrival, the railroad, shoe.

The words, like bees in a sweet ink, cluster and drone,
Indifferent, indelible,
A hum and a hum:
Back stairsteps to God, ropes to the glass eye:
Vineyard, informer, the chair, the throne.

Mojo and numberless, breaths
From the wet mountains and green mouths; rustlings,
Sure sleights of hand,
The news that arrives from nowhere:
Angel, omega, silence, silence . . .

*1945*

13.

What I remember is fire, orange fire,
And his huge cock in his hand,
Touching my tiny one; the smell
Of coal dust, the smell of heat,
Banked flames through the furnace door.

Of him I remember little, if anything:
Black, overalls splotched with soot,
His voice, *honey, O, honey* . . .
And then he came, his left hand
On my back, holding me close.

Nothing was said, of course — one
Terrible admonition, and that was all . . .
And if that hand, like loosed lumber, fell
From grace, and stayed there? We give,
And we take it back. We give again . . .

*1940*

14.

Now there is one, and still masked;
White death's face, sheeted and shoeless, eyes shut
Behind the skull holes.
She stands in a field, her shadow no shadow,
The clouds no clouds. Call her Untitled.

\*

And now there are four, white shoes, white socks;
They stand in the same field, the same clouds
Vanishing down the sky. Cat masks and mop hair
Cover their faces. Advancing, they hold hands.

\*

Nine. Now there are nine, their true shadows
The judgments beneath their feet.
Black masks, white nightgowns. A wind
Is what calls them, that field, those same clouds
Lisping one syllable *I, I, I.*

*1970*

15.

And the saw keeps cutting,
Its flashy teeth shredding the mattress, the bedclothes,
The pillow and pillow case.
Plugged in to a socket in your bones,
It coughs, and keeps on cutting.

It eats the lamp and the bedpost.
It licks the clock with its oiled tongue,
And keeps on cutting.
It leaves the bedroom, and keeps on cutting.
It leaves the house, and keeps on cutting . . .

— Dogwood, old feathery petals,
Your black notches burn in my blood;
You flutter like bandages across my childhood.
Your sound is a sound of good-bye.
Your poem is a poem of pain.

*1964*

16.

All gloss, gothic and garrulous, staked
To her own tree, she takes it off,
Half-dollar an article. With each
Hike of the price, the gawkers
Diminish, spitting, rubbing their necks.

Fifteen, and staked to *my* tree,
Sap-handled, hand in my pocket, head
Hot as the carnival tent, I see it out — as does
The sheriff of Cherokee County,
Who fondles the payoff, finger and shaft.

Outside, in the gathering dark, all
Is fly buzz and gnat hum and whine of the wires;
Quick scratch of the match, cicadas,
Jackhammer insects; drone, drone
Of the blood-suckers, sweet dust, last sounds . . .

*1950*

17.

I dream that I dream I wake
The room is throat-deep and brown with dead moths
I throw them back like a quilt
I peel them down from the wall
I kick them like leaves I shake them I kick them again

The bride on the couch and the bridegroom
Under their gauze dust-sheet
And cover up turn to each other
Top hat and tails white veil and say as I pass
*It's mother again just mother* the window open

On the 10th floor going up
Is Faceless and under steam his mask
Hot-wired my breath at his heels in sharp clumps
Darkness and light darkness and light
Faceless come back O come back

*1955 ff.*

18.

Flash click tick, flash click tick, light
Through the wavefall — electrodes, intolerable curlicues;
Splinters along the skin, eyes
Flicked by the sealash, spun, pricked;
Terrible vowels from the sun.

And everything dry, wrung, the land flaked
By the wind, bone dust and shale;
And hills without names or numbers,
Bald coves where the sky harbors.
The dead grass whistles a tune, strangely familiar.

And all in a row, seated, their mouths biting the empty air,
Their front legs straight, and their backs straight,
Their bodies pitted, eyes wide,
The rubble quick glint beneath their feet,
The lions stare, explaining it one more time.

*1959*

19.

The hemlocks wedge in the wind.
Their webs are forming something—questions:
*Which shoe is the alter ego?*
*Which glove inures the fallible hand?*
*Why are the apple trees in draped black?*

And I answer them. In words
They will understand, I answer them:
*The left shoe.*
*The left glove.*
*Someone is dead; someone who loved them is dead.*

Regret is what anchors me;
I wash in a water of odd names.
White flakes from next year sift down, sift down.
I lie still, and dig in,
Snow-rooted, ooze-rooted, cold blossom.

*1972*

20.

You stand in your shoes, two shiny graves
Dogging your footsteps;
You spread your fingers, ten stalks
Enclosing your right of way;
You yip with pain in your little mouth.

And this is where the ash falls.
And this is the time it took to get here—
And yours, too, is the stall, the wet wings
Arriving, and the beak.
And yours the thump, and the soft voice:

The octopus on the reef's edge, who slides
His fat fingers among the cracks,
Can use you. You've prayed to him,
In fact, and don't know it.
You *are* him, and think yourself yourself.

*1973*

## Notes to Tattoos

1. Camellias; Mother's Day; St Paul's Episcopal Church, Kingsport, Tennessee.
2. Death of my father.
3. Snake-handling religious service; East Tennessee.
4. Venice, Italy.
5. Acolyte; fainting at the altar; Kingsport, Tennessee.
6. Blood-poisoning; hallucination; Hiwassee, North Carolina.
7. *The Resurrection*, Piero della Francesca; Borgo San Sepolcro, Italy.
8. Harold Schimmel's morning prayers; Positano, Italy.
9. Temporary evangelical certitude; Christ School, Arden, North Carolina.
10. Visions of heaven.
11. Automobile wreck; hospital; Baltimore, Maryland.
12. Handwriting class; Palmer Method; words as 'things'; Kingsport, Tennessee.
13. The janitor; kindergarten; Corinth, Mississippi.
14. Dream.
15. The day of my mother's funeral, in Tennessee; Rome, Italy.
16. Sideshow stripper; Cherokee County Fair, Cherokee, North Carolina.
17. Recurrent dream.
18. The Naxian lions; Delos, Greece.
19. Death of my father.
20. The last stanza is an adaptation of lines from Eugenio Montale's *Serenata Indiana*.

3.

## Hardin County

—CPW, 1904–1972

There are birds that are parts of speech, bones
That are suns in the quick earth.
There are ice floes that die of cold.
There are rivers with many doors, and names
That pull their thread from their own skins.
Your grief was something like this.

Or self-pity, I might add, as you did
When you were afraid to sleep,
And not sleep, afraid to touch your bare palm;
Afraid of the wooden dog, the rose
Bleating beside your nightstand; afraid
Of the slur in the May wind.

It wasn't always like that, not in those first years
When the moon went on without its waters,
When the cores blew out of their graves in Hardin County.
How useless it is to cry out, to try
And track that light, now
Reduced to a grain of salt in the salt snow.

I want the dirt to go loose, the east wind
To pivot and fold like a string.
I want the pencil to eat its words,
The star to be sucked through its black hole.
And everything stays the same,
Locks unpicked, shavings unswept on the stone floor.

The grass reissues its green music; the leaves
Of the sassafras tree take it and pass it on;
The sunlight scatters its small change.
The dew falls, the birds smudge on their limbs.
And, over Oak Hill, the clouds, those mansions of nothingness,
Keep to their own appointments, and hurry by.

## Delta Traveller

—MWW, 1910–1964

Born in the quarter-night, brash
Tongue on the tongueless ward, the moon down,
The lake rising on schedule and Dr Hurt
Already across the water, and headed home —
And so I came sailing out, first child,
A stream with no bed to lie in,
A root with no branch to leaf,
The black balloon of promise tied to your wrist,
One inch of pain and an inch of light.

*

No wonder the children stand by those moist graves.
And produce is spread on the cobbled streets,
And portraits are carried out, and horns play.
And women, in single file, untangle
Corn from the storage bins, and soft cheese.
I shield my eyes against the sunlight,
Holding, in one hand, a death's-head,
Spun sugar and marzipan. I call it Love,
And shield my eyes against the sunlight.

*

I lie down with you, I rise up with you.
If a grain turns in my eye,
I know it is you, entering, leaving,
Your name like a lozenge upon my tongue.
You drift through the antilife,
Scrim and snow-scud, fluff stem, hair
And tendril. You bloom in your own throat,
Frost flame in the frost dust,
One scratch on the slipstream, a closed mouth.

45

High-necked and high-collared, slumped and creased,
A dress sits in a chair. Your dress,
Or your mother's dress, a dress
On a wooden chair, in a cold room, a room
With no windows and no doors, full of the east wind.
The dress gets up, windbone and windskin,
To open the window. It is not there.
It goes to the door. It is not there.
The dress goes back and sits down. The dress gets up . . .

*

Three teeth and a thumbnail, white, white; four
Fingers that cradle a black chin;
Outline of eye-hole and nose-hole. This skull
And its one hand float up from the tar
And lime pit of dreams, night after slick night,
To lodge in the fork of the gum tree,
Its three teeth in the leaflight,
Its thumbnail in flash and foil,
Its mouth-hole a nothing I need to know.

*

Cat's-eye and cloud, you survive.
The porcelain corridors
That glide forever beneath your feet,
The armed lawn chair you sit in,
Your bones like paint, your skin the wrong color—
All this you survive, and hold on,
A way of remembering, a pulse
That comes and goes in the night,
Match flare and wink, that comes and goes in the night.

*

If the wafer of light offends me,
 If the split tongue in the snake's mouth offends me,
I am not listening. They make the sound,
Which is the same sound, of the ant hill,
The hollow trunk, the fruit of the tree.
It is the Echo, the one transmitter of things:
Transcendent and inescapable,
It is the cloud, the mosquito's buzz,
The trickle of water across the leaf's vein.

*

And so with the dead, the rock dead and the dust:
Worm and worm-fill, pearl, milk-eye
And light in the earth, the dead are brought
Back to us, piece by piece—
Under the sponged log, inside the stump,
They shine with their secret lives, and grow
Big with their messages, wings
Beginning to stir, paths fixed and hearts clocked,
Rising and falling back and rising.

**4.**

# Skins

1.

Whatever furrow you dig in the red earth,
Whatever the tree you hang your lights on,
There comes that moment
When what you are is what you will be
Until the end, no matter
What prayer you answer to—a life
Of margins, white of the apple, white of the eye,
No matter how long you hold your hands out.
You glance back and you glance back. Ahead, in the distance, a cry
Skreeks like a chalk on a blackboard.
Through riprap or backfill, sandstone or tidedrift,
You go where the landshed takes you,
One word at a time, still
Counting your money, wearing impermanent clothes.

2.

In the brushstroke that holds the angel's wing
Back from perfection; in
The synapse of word to word; in the one note
That would strike the infinite ear
And save you; and in
That last leap, the sure and redeeming edge . . .
In all beauty there lies
Something inhuman, something you can't know:
In the pith and marrow of every root
Of every bloom; in the blood-seam
Of every rock; in the black lung of every cloud
The seed, the infinitesimal seed
That dooms you, that makes you nothing,
Feeds on its self-containment and grows big.

3.

And here is the ledge,
A white ledge on a blue scarp, blue sky
Inseparable in the definition; a lens
Is tracking inexorably toward you.
Your shadow trails like a train
For miles down the glacierside, your face into view
Obliquely, then not at all,
Eyes thumbed, lips like pieces of cut glass:
This is the fair print:
Take it, eat it, it is your body and blood,
Your pose and your sacrifice; it is
Your greed and your sustenance . . .
The lens retracks, the shot unmistakable.
Take it, and be glad.

4.

First came geometry, and its dish of sparks,
Then the indifferent blue.
Then God, Original Dread, Old Voodoo Wool,
Lock-step and shadow-sprung,
Immense in the oily wind . . .
Later, the gatherings: ice, dust and its fiery hair,
The seeds in their endless scattering . . .
This linkage is nondescript
But continuing, the stars drifting into the cold
Like the corpses of Borneo
Set forth on their own rafts, washing into oblivion;
Like the reliquary tears
Of prophets, falling and falling away,
Back to geometry, back to its dish of ash.

5.

Nevertheless, the wheel arcs; nevertheless,
The mud slides and the arms yearn;
Nevertheless, you turn your face
Toward the black stone, the hard breath on the lip of God,
And find cloud, the clot you can't swallow,
The wishbone you can't spit out.
And move on, to the great fall of water;
And the light that moves there, and the click:
In the shallows, the insects,
Quick kernels of darkness, pale and explain themselves; newts
Shuttle their lanterns through the glassy leaves;
The crayfish open their doors;
The drenched wings of sunclusters rise
Like thousands of tiny cathedrals into their new language . . .

6.

Under the rock, in the sand and the gravel run;
In muck bank and weed, at the heart of the river's edge:
Instar; and again, instar,
The wing cases visible. Then
Emergence: leaf drift and detritus; skin split,
The image forced from the self.
And rests, wings drying, eyes compressed,
Legs compressed, constricted
Beneath the dun and the watershine—
Incipient spinner, set for the take-off . . .
And does, in clean tear: imago rising out of herself
For the last time, slate-winged and many-eyed.
And joins, and drops to her destiny,
Flesh to the surface, wings flush on the slate film.

7.

Sucked in and sucked out, tidewash
Hustles its razzmatazz across the cut lips
Of coral, the thousands of tiny punctures
Spewing and disappearing . . .
Where is that grain of sand that Blake saw,
The starfish that lights the way?
Pools and anemones open and close . . .
And now, on the sea's black floor,
A hand is turning your card,
One card, one turn: two dogs bark at the moon;
The crab resets her glass clock.
The weight of the sea
Is killing: you pack it forever. Shift it, sluff it;
You pack it, blue mother, forever.

8.

Something has grazed your cheek, your foot and your fingertips:
The tedious scarf of sleep, adrift
Through the afternoon. At one end, a lizard
Darts from a red rock into shade;
At the other, birds rise in the rank, inveterate blue.
July, and the olive is silhouette. The lake
Shrugs its shoulders, and goes on
Slapping its palms on the wet shale, goes on
Washing its laundry. Under
The fish-silver flash of the olive leaves, poppies
Crane up with their one good eye, and do
Nothing; the bees drag their yellow slumber.
Small pleasures: the poor man's pickpurse, the rich man's cutthroat.
Grainout . . . And so what? You're only passing through.

9.

The earth is what salivates, what sticks like a new glue.
It is to walk on, it is to lie down in,
A sure sheet for the resurrection.
The earth is what follows you,
Tracing your footsteps, counting your teeth, father
And son, father and grandson,
A knife, a seed, each planted just deep enough.
You start there. The birds from your sleeve burst into flame;
Your shoes catch fire, your good shoes;
Your socks sink in the dirt, all pain gone;
Your ankles sink in the dirt, your shinbones, your legs . . .
Necessity's after-breeder,
Inflamed like asparagus in the night field,
You try for the get-away by the light of yourself.

10.

Androgynous tincture, *prima materia*;
The quintessential reprieve
And coupling: sod-lifting, folly and light
In the crucible, and in the air;
And in the crosswinds, the details of diffidence . . .
This is the stung condition, and silencer:
To have come this far, to have got the jump,
The radiant archipelagos
From fog into fog beneath your body streaming—
And abstract from this
Fabric, this silkscreen that patterns you
(The chancelled dawn, vast
Surplice and undershine), one glint of the golden stitch,
The thread that will lead you home:

11.

Upriver, then, past landfall and watertrace,
Past wheels, past time and its bufferings . . .
A clearing appears; reed huts
Extend from the jungle face, its vinelap and overbite;
Out of them step, in cadence—a slip skip slip—,
Two men with their six-foot flutes, two women behind them,
Their dance, their song ascending like smoke and light
Back to the sky, back to the place it came from . . .
Of course, it's unworkable.
Better to dig a round hole in the earth, be lowered
And fixed in the clay in a stranger's arms;
Be covered with thick feathers,
Your stiff arms stiff at your sides, knees flexed,
Marked for the tilt and the blind slide.

12.

*Exurgent mortui et ad me veniunt . . . :*
Midnight, the Christmas Mass; and the host raised, and the summoned
Summoned. And then to the boneyard, eyes eastward,
Two bones in the right hand, St Andrew's cross
Pathetic against the dawn's skull.
Then north, four thousand and nineteen hundred paces,
To lie down, outstretched, hands on the legs,
Eyes heavenward, unlocked to the quarter moon:
*Ego sum, te peto et videre queo . . .*
And will they step from their dust?
Will they sit in their rocking chairs, decayed hands
Explaining the maps you must follow?
Will circles be explicated, the signs shriven?
The land of the chosen has one door; there is no knob . . .

13.

Naked, spindled, the hand on the chimney mantel,
Length-fingered, bud-sprouted bone:
The Hand of Glory, spread toward its one address:
The right hand, or the left hand,
Lopped at the new moon, and fresh from the gibbet;
Wrapped in a funeral pall, squeezed, palmed;
Then brought, in the dog-days, from its pot,
Pumiced by zimat, nitre and long peppers;
Then to the oven; vervain
And fern imbue its grainlessness; the candle
— Man-fat, wax, ponie and sesame —
Forks from its wonder; lighted,
It freezes the looker's reach, and locks both
The mark and beholder, ghost forms on the negative . . .

14.

They talk of a city, whose moon-colored battlements
Kneel to the traveller, whose
Windows, like after-burners, stream
Out their chemistry, applying their anodyne.
They talk of a river, its waters
A balm, an unguent unscrubbable. They talk. And they talk
Of the light that lights the stars
Through the five organs, like a wind spread by the rain.
They talk of a medicine, a speck
— Omnipotent, omnipresent, clogged
With the heavy earth and the mind's intractable screen —
To be shaken loose, dissolved, and blown
Through the veins, becoming celestial.
They talk, and nothing appears. They talk and it does not appear.

15.

And so downriver, yourself, and yourself's shadow,
All that you bring back.
Still, it's enough: sounding board, handhold,
Ear-rig and in-seeing eye . . .
Back from the seven-caved mountain, its cross
Where the serpent is nailed; back
From the oak-stock and rose, their rivulet
Sought by the blind with their dry touch; back
From the Innocents, that vat where the sun and the moon
Dip to their red bath . . .
The Echo is arbitrary: flame, wind, rainwrack
And soil; each a survivor, each one
An heir to the fingerprint, the slip of a tongue.
Each is where you begin; each one an end in itself . . .

16.

Procedure and process, the one
Inalterable circulation. First, cleared ground, swept
And unhindered; next, bark moss, pine pitch,
Their angles of termination
Exact, the boughs that are added exact; then loblolly, split
From the fall felling; then ball bats, blue shoes,
All the paraphernalia of past lives:
The headrests, the backrests, all the poor furniture . . .
As the fire builds, you enter and lie down:
You feed the flames; you feed them with all you've got:
Finger and forearm, torso,
Shoulders and hair . . . And the sparks
That rise, the cinders,
Rework you and make you new, burned to an ash.

17.

The wind hauls out its valued baggage in three steps
Tonight, and drops it with some relief
In the full dark, in the leaves of an avocado tree.
The grass rises to meet it.
As always, you, too, rise, and meet them halfway,
And nod your head, and accept
Their leavings, and give thanks, crumbs
For the tablecloth, crumbs for the plate, and wolf them down . . .
The rivers of air you've filtered and rearranged
Since birth, and paid no heed to,
Surprise you now, and start to take on
The acid and eye of what's clear,
That milky message of breath on cold mornings—
That what you take in is seldom what you let out.

18.

There is a shine you move towards, the shine
Of water; you want it to step from,
And out of, wearing its strings and slick confetti.
You come to the sea, but turn back, its surgy retractions
Too slippery, and out of place,
Wrecked looking-glass, bundles of grief.
And inland, the necklace of lakes — High Lonesome
And pendant, the 40s its throat,
Its glint like icicles against the skin . . . ?
There's no one to wear it now, or hand it down.
The river will have it, shine
Of the underlight, shine of the lost quarter;
The river, rope of remembering, unbroken shoe,
The flushed and unwaivering mirror . . .

19.

You thought you climbed, and all the while you descended.
Go up and go down; what other work is there
For you to do, what other work in this world?
The seasons back off. The hills
Debase themselves, and keep on growing. Over the land,
Your feet touch down like feathers,
A brushstroke here, a gouge there, lacking a print
Always, and always without direction.
Or so it seems. But what, for one meandering man,
Is all that, who looks for the willow's change,
The drift and slip of smoke through the poplar leaves,
The cliff's dance and wind's shift,
Alone with the owl and the night crawler
Where all is a true turning, and all is growth.

20.

You've talked to the sun and moon,
Those idols of stitched skin, bunch grass and twigs
Stuck on their poles in the fall rain;
You've prayed to Sweet Medicine;
You've looked at the Hanging Road, its stars
The stepstones and river bed where you hope to cross;
You've followed the cricket's horn
To sidestep the Lake of Pain . . .
And what does it come to, Pilgrim,
This walking to and fro on the earth, knowing
That nothing changes, or everything;
And only, to tell it, these sad marks,
Phrases half-parsed, ellipses and scratches across the dirt?
It comes to a point. It comes and it goes.

5.

## Link Chain

Palm Sunday. Banana leaves
Loll in the breaklight. Back home, on Ravine Street
25 years ago, Philbeck and I
Would count the crosses, arrange
The pins on their silver plate, and bank
On a full house. The palm crosses, tiny
And off-green against their purple cloth,
Are stacked like ricks for the match flame. 11 o'clock.
I take a cross and two pins —
One for the cross, and one again for the heart.

*

On the front seat of a Yellow Coach,
Pistol Red at the wheel, 10 miles this side of Surgoinsville
On US 11-W, I'd lay my body down, in Tennessee,
For the 1st time. The 2nd time
I'd pick a tree, black cherry,
That grows on the north side of Chestnut Ridge, and looks out
Over the Cumberlands;
I'd build a floor and face west.
For number 3, I'd float in a boat downriver,
Whatever river, and be a leaf.

*

Circle by circle, link chain
And hair breath, I'm bound to the oak mulch, those leaves
Stuffed in their croker sacks
My brother and I were sent for each week-end
In autumn, in Moody's Woods, to drag back

Up Hog Hill and feed the shredder with.
Later, confettied and packed tight in their little mounds,
They warmed the milk root and the slip stalk.
Later still, and less coarse, they'll warm me,
Bone stock and finger peg, the cold room.

*

From this pocket to that pocket, bright coin
Whose slot in the crossed box was cut
38 years ago, and cut well,
I roll through the world, Peter's pence
For the red clay, defrocked and worn smooth,
The payment in someone's hand.
Lord of the Anchorite, wind-blown bird,
Dangle your strings and hook me.
I am the gleam in your good eye, I am your ticket;
Take me up, and drop me where I belong.

*

Each tree I look at contains my coffin,
Each train brings it closer home.
Each flower I cut, I cut for a plastic vase
Askew on the red dirt, the oak trees
Whisking their wash in the May wind.
Each root I uncover uncovers me.
Below, 19 By-pass swings straight to the state line
5 miles north, Virginia across the bridge —
Each car is the car that brings
That tree to earth, the earth to the earth again.

*

Big Sister, hair heaped like a fresh grave,
Turns in my arms as my arms turn,
Her fingers cool tubers against my skin

As we slide slide to the music, humming
An old tune, knee touching knee,
Step-two-three, step-two-three
Under a hard hatful of leaves,
The grass with its one good limb holding
The beat, a hint of impending form.
It gathers, it reaches back, it is caught up.

## Bays Mountain Covenant

For my own speech and that which I leave unspoken
For my own death and the deaths that will follow me
For the three thrones for the sticks for the wires
For the whole hog and the half-truth
For my knot of life and its one string
That goes from this man's rumor to that one's promise
For the songs I hear and the hush I should imitate
For the sky my eye sees and the one that it cannot find
For the raising up and the setting down
For the light for the light for the light

He praised for 10 years and was suckered by
A foot in the wrong shoe a hat in the wind
Sir you will pardon him you will wave if he now turns
To the leaf to the fire in the swamp log to the rain
The acorn of crystal at the creek's edge which prove
Nothing expect nothing and offer nothing
Desire no entrance and harbor no hope of change
Foxglove that seeks no answer nightshade that seeks no answer
Not to arrive at and be part of but to take
As the water accepts the whirlpool the earth the storm

## Rural Route

The stars come out to graze, wild-eyed in the new dark.
The dead squeeze close together,
Strung out like a seam of coal through the raw earth.
I smell its fragrance, I touch its velvet walls.

The willow lets down her hooks.
On the holly leaves, the smears of light
Retrench and repeat their alphabet,
That slow code. The boxwood leans out to take it on,

Quicker, but still unbroken.
Inside the house, in one room, a twelve-year-old
Looks at his face on the windowpane, a face
Once mine, the same twitch to the eye.

The willow flashes her hooks.
I step closer. Azalea branches and box snags
Drag at my pants leg, twenty-six years gone by.
I enter the wedge of light.

And the face stays on the window, the eyes unchanged.
It still looks in, still unaware of the willow, the boxwood
Or any light on any leaf. Or me.
Somewhere a tire squeals, somewhere a door is shut twice.

And what it sees is what it has always seen:
Stuffed birds on a desk top, a deer head
On the wall, and all the small things we used once
To push the twelve rings of the night back.

How silly! And still they call us
Across the decades, fog horns,
Not destinations; outposts of things to avoid, reefs
To steer clear of, pockets of great abandon.

I back off, and the face stays.
I leave the back yard, and the front yard, and the face stays.
I am back on the West Coast, in my studio,
My wife and my son asleep, and the face stays.